WHO IS THE TRUE GOD?

By
J. Paul Reno
Pastor and Author

WHO IS THE TRUE GOD?

Copyrighted © by J. Paul Reno
June, 2017

ISBN: 978-0-9987778-3-2

Published by
Blessed Hope Publishers
Hagerstown, Maryland
June, 2017

All Scripture quotations in this book are taken from the *King James Version* of the Bible.

Publishing and Formatting Assisted by
The Old Paths Publications
142 Gold Flume Way
Cleveland, GA 30528
Web address: www.theoldpathspublications.com
Email address: TOP@theoldpathspublications.com
www.theoldpathspublications.com
TOP@theoldpathspublications.com

"All scripture is given by inspiration of God, and is profitable for doctrine, for reproof, for correction, for instruction in righteousness.

That the man of God may be perfect, throughly furnished unto all good works."

(II Tim. 3:16, 17)

DEDICATION

"I want to dedicate this book to Edgar Thomas, Bob Doom and Ray Bearden who preached evangelistically, presenting the True God to both saint and sinner. I want to also dedicate it to the many pastors, missionaries, evangelists and Bible teachers who faithfully present the True God to this confused and compromising generation. May their efforts deliver us from this form of godliness that lacks reality."

Pastor J. Paul Reno

WHO IS THE TRUE GOD?

TABLE OF CONTENTS

DEDICATION 3
TABLE OF CONTENTS 5
INTRODUCTION 7
CHAPTER 1: GOD REVEALS HIMSELF 11
   God is everywhere. 13
CHAPTER 2: GOD IS TRIUNE 27
CHAPTER 3: GOD IS HOLY 39
CHAPTER 4: GOD IS LOVE 59
CHAPTER 5: GOD IS MIGHTY 65
CHAPTER 6: GOD GIVES COMMANDS 79
CHAPTER 7: GOD HAS CHILDREN 87
INDEX OF WORDS AND PHRASES 100
ABOUT THE AUTHOR 106

WHO IS THE TRUE GOD?

INTRODUCTION

We don't have to go far in the Bible before we find a false idea of God. In **Genesis chapter 3**, the devil told Eve she could become like the gods. She fell for that temptation. A lot of people fall for the temptation to become like the gods they worship--false gods instead of the true God. **I John 5:21** states, *"Little children, keep yourselves from idols. Amen."* We are to stay away from that which is false--physical, mental, or emotional idolatry that pictures a god who is not the true God. We want the true God, and we need to know who He is.

Who is the true God? This issue is becoming bigger and bigger in America. So-called Christian groups no longer agree on Who God is. America is swarming with cults that we can't call Christian. Religions are flooding into our country presenting a god who is different than the true God. The Mormons say that Jesus is the brother of the devil and that God the Father used to be a man like we are. Most Seventh Day Adventists and Jehovah's Witnesses believe that Jesus was an angel. The Christian Scientists believe that love is God--not God is love. If you have love, that is God. All these groups have a different god than the true God of the Bible. The Muslims say Allah is God. Their Allah is not the true God of the Bible. Yet, we have people who act like he is the same God but just worshipped a little differently. The true God is different than the multitudes of gods of the Hindus or the gods of the Buddhists and Confucians.

The true God is portrayed from **Genesis 1:1** all the way to the end of **Revelation.** If we read through the Bible once a year, we get one opportunity to see the entire portrayal. However, God put the details we need to get started in five short chapters. We can read **I John** through in fifteen or twenty minutes. We can easily read it twice a day and day after day to let the truth sink in. **Who is the true God?**

The book of **I John** has two major themes. They are laid out for us in **I John 5:20,**

> ***"And we know that the*** *Son of God is come, and hath given us an understanding, that we may know him that is true, and we are in him that is true, even in his Son Jesus Christ. This is the true God, and eternal life."*

One major theme is **"eternal life."** We can study through the book of **I John** and find 12 marks or evidences of eternal life. These marks can be used to

INTRODUCTION

evaluate whether a person really has eternal life. Many say they have it, but have no evidences of it. **I John** was written that we might know what eternal life is and whether we have it.

The other major theme of **I John** is "**This is the true God**." When God says, **"This is the true God,"** He implies that all other gods are false. Many people have a false god. They may think they know Who God is, but they really don't. Some have misunderstood, and others have been taught falsehoods about God. Theirs is a wrong view of God or a misshapen or partial view of God. They get into all kinds of trouble because they don't know Who God is. We need to know Who the true God is. **I John** is a short book that speaks eloquently and repeatedly on this subject. It makes it very clear that there is a difference between the true God and all other gods. What are the marks of distinction so that we can defend ourselves against error and help others to know Who the true God is?

J. Paul Reno

CHAPTER 1

GOD REVEALS HIMSELF

God wants us to know Him. We can't figure Him out or study Him out, but He reveals Himself so that we can know Who He is. He reveals and manifests Himself in ways that He explains to us. We might learn a few facts about God and accept them because someone taught them. However, when God Himself reveals the truth to us, we get to know Him; and there are no doubts. People can raise other issues and try to sidetrack us on Who God is, but we know the true God because He has revealed Himself to us.

We don't see God because by nature He is invisible and not viewable. Jesus told the Samaritan woman that God is a Spirit. **I John 4:12a** says, "***No man hath seen God at any time.***" We can't see Him with our eyes, our mind, or our imagination. We need to understand this. If God is going to reveal Himself, He is not going to reveal Himself in a blaze of light by our bedside. Most of us have heard people say that God came and visited them by their bed one night. What those people saw was not the true God. Some say they have seen artist's pictures of God. An artist's picture is not the true God. God is invisible by nature because He is a spirit being. Let this sink in, and watch how it will correct a whole lot of error. According to the Bible, we can have idols in our hearts as well as on the shelf. We are to keep ourselves from idols (**I John 5:21**).

I John 1:10 says,

> *"If we say that we have not sinned, we make him a liar, and his word is not in us."*

God didn't give us His Word as the words of man but as His Word. He didn't give it to us to keep on a shelf or coffee table or just to carry in and out of a church house. God gave us His Word to actually soak down into our souls. His Word is not just to be around us or carried by us. His Word is to be in us. We need to let the Word of God saturate our being. God reveals Himself; and one of the ways He does is by and through His Word. A lot of people that talk about knowing God don't read the Bible. Even less do they let the Word of God saturate them.

I remember visiting in the home of a man whose marriage was about to break up. He had a drinking and drug problem. His family asked if I would spend time talking to him to see if anything could be done. I went, and he was willing to sit there and listen to me. Finally, after I had made a weekly visit of about an hour for several months, I began talking about God; and he told me he believed in God. He said he knew all about God. That was a revelation to me! I asked him what he knew about Him. (I was kind enough not to take my watch out to time him.) He repeated himself several times in less than thirty seconds. He said, "Everybody knows about God.

God is everywhere.

I know about God. He is everywhere." Finally, he asked me to tell him about God. That was what I had been waiting for.

It takes the Word of God to reveal God. This man thought he knew Him because he knew a few terms. He didn't know God. God hadn't made Himself clear to him. The man had never really focused on the Word of God or let it soak into him. He finally understood that the Bible needed to be read, studied, and pondered. He needed to let God's Word affect his life. We all need to understand the importance of the Word of God because that is one of the ways God reveals Himself.

I John 2:3, 4 says,

"And hereby we do know that we know him, if we keep his commandments. He that saith, I know him, and keepeth not his commandments, is a liar, and the truth is not in him."

God gave commandments, and we can learn to know God by His commandments.

"Be ye holy; for I am holy" (I Peter 1:16). "Thou shalt not bear false witness" (Ex. 20:16).

Looking at His commands, we know something about Him. If we avoid His Word and His commands, we will be ignorant about many things of God.

Many people are chasing a god other than the true God. Alcoholics Anonymous was started by a group of spiritists. They say we worship god as we conceive him to be. That is a god as big as our imagination and no bigger. We have a God that reveals Himself through **HIS** Word and commandments. That is how He shows Who He is. We can read the Koran, but we will not find God because neither God's Word nor God's commands are in the Koran. We can read other religious books and other things people write. We can listen to what people say. However, if people's writings

CHAPTER 1: GOD REVEALS HIMSELF

or people's words don't have God's Words and God's commandments, we are going to miss out on much of Who God is.

Another of the ways God reveals Himself is in salvation. When God saves us, we get to know some things about Him. We may read those things later, and we recognize them as truth. Sometimes people get saved without all the teaching and preaching they perhaps should have had. However, when they get saved, God confirms truth about Himself to their hearts.

When God saves a sinner, knowledge comes that is foundational for all Christian growth and experience thereafter. There are three levels in saved people spiritually--children, young men, and fathers. All three have that foundational knowledge of God. **I John 2:13-14** says,

> *"I write unto you, fathers, because ye have known him that is from the beginning. I write unto you, young men, because ye have overcome the wicked one. I write unto you, little children, because ye have known the Father. I have written unto you, fathers, because ye*

have known him that is from the beginning. I have written unto you, young men, because ye are strong, and the Word of God abideth in you, and ye have overcome the wicked one."

Let me quote from Jesus' high priestly prayer in **John 17:3**,

"And this is life eternal, that they might know thee the only true God, and Jesus Christ, whom thou hast sent."

Salvation involves knowledge of God. Salvation brings a revelation of God to man in a practical way-- down in the soul. People who don't know the true God aren't saved.

I John 1:3, 6-7 reads,

"That which we have seen and heard declare we unto you, that ye also may have fellowship with us: and truly our fellowship is with the Father, and with his Son Jesus Christ. If we say that we have fellowship with him, and walk in darkness, we lie, and do not the truth: But if we walk in the light, as he is in the light,

CHAPTER 1: GOD REVEALS HIMSELF

we have fellowship one with another, and the blood of Jesus Christ his Son cleanseth us from all sin."

God reveals Himself in fellowship. This is what Enoch experienced and what we ought to enjoy too--fellowshipping with the Father and with the Son. I am talking about a practical revelation. Fellowship is not something we memorize, a creed we accept, or facts we learn. Fellowship is experientially getting to know the true God. He fellowships and spends time with His people. We are to spend time with Him. We know Him through fellowship.

I John 2:15-17 states,

"Love not the world, neither the things that are in the world. If any man love the world, the love of the Father is not in him. For all that is in the world, the lust of the flesh, and the lust of the eyes, and the pride of life, is not of the Father, but is of the world. And the world passeth away, and the lust thereof: but he that doeth the will of God abideth for ever."

"If any man love the world, the love of the Father is not in him."

We can't love both the world and God. When we look at the world, we see something that is the opposite of Who God is. When we look at God and get to know Him, we see something that is the opposite of what the world is. The idea of the "worldly Christian" is a contradiction of terms. Great contrast and very clear distinctions separate God and the world! If we know God, we are going to hate the world. If we love the world, we won't want God. It is that simple. A person who loves God will not walk step by step with someone who is in love with the world. In the book of **James**, God called those that love the world adulterers and adulteresses.

Thus, if we want to learn something about God, we see what the world is. The world is exactly what God isn't. The world feeds the lust of the flesh, the lust of the eyes, and the pride of life. God won't. God will make us humble. God will attune us to the eternal. God will direct us in a right path. He is different from the god that is presented in most so-called Christian, evangelical, and in some cases, fundamental churches today. This is the true God of the Bible.

I John 1:1-3a reads,

CHAPTER 1: GOD REVEALS HIMSELF

"That which was from the beginning, which we have heard, which we have seen with our eyes, which we have looked upon, and our hands have handled, of the Word of life; (For the life was manifested, and we have seen it, and bear witness, and shew unto you that eternal life, which was with the Father, and was manifested unto us;) That which we have seen and heard declare we unto you, that ye also may have fellowship with us."

God sent His Son Jesus Christ by means of the incarnation that we might know the true God--the Lord Jesus Christ. The true God became a man--eternal life personified and deity mixed with humanity. John says the disciples saw Him and handled Him (**I John 1:1**). John wanted to show us and tell us what the disciples had a chance to see. Through the Teacher within and the Word recorded, God can reveal Himself to us as clearly as He was revealed through Jesus to those disciples. God can become just as real, just as known, and just as recognized. This is a marvelous thing!

I John 2:5, 6 says,

> *"But whoso keepeth his word, in him verily is the love of God perfected: hereby know we that we are in him. He that saith he abideth in him ought himself also to walk even as He walked."*

Jesus came as an infant and grew up through childhood, youth, and adult years. He:

> *"was in all points tempted like as we are, yet without sin" (Hebrews 4:15b).*

Jesus set an example for us.

By following Him, we may know the true God and see how to walk as the true God would have us to walk. Jesus was more than just an example, but He was an example. We are to walk in His steps. We get to know God as we walk that pathway. We will need to pray to God, depend on Him, and cry out to Him for help as we walk along. The closer we get to Jesus, the more real the true God becomes.

I John 3:8 states,

> *"He that committeth sin is of the devil; for the devil sinneth from the beginning. For this purpose the Son of*

God was manifested, that he might destroy the works of the devil."

God sent His Son and had Him revealed and manifested to destroy the very works of the devil.

I John 3:5 says,

"And ye know that he was manifested to take away our sins; and in him is no sin."

Jesus destroyed Satan's works. Watch Him as He takes away sins. Do you remember the moment when God, manifest through Jesus, made Himself so real that the terrible load of guilt and the weight of your sins was taken away? Jesus doesn't just forgive us, He takes our sins away.

"... Thou shalt call his name JESUS for he shall save his people FROM their sins" (Matt. 1:21b).

God is the God Who washes us and cleanses us from our sins through Jesus. God reveals Himself as He destroys the devil's works in my life and your life and the lives of those around us. We have a God Who can pull down and destroy all that the devil might try to do. The devil can't build anything that God can't tear down, but our God has much that the devil can't tear down. Any work the devil is doing can't stand when God moves on the scene. That is the true God of the Bible. He is not defeated by the devil, but rather the devil is defeated by Him.

I John 4:2, 3a reads,

"Hereby know ye the Spirit of God: Every spirit that confesseth that Jesus Christ is come in the flesh is of God: And every spirit that confesseth not that Jesus Christ is come in the flesh is not of God: and this is that spirit of antichrist,"

The issue isn't whether Jesus existed, but rather whether Jesus pre-existed Bethlehem and then came in the flesh. Jesus makes Himself known as we realize,

"...without him was not any thing made that was made" (John 1:3b).

Jesus created. He was there at creation. He said,

"Before Abraham was, I am." (John 8:58b).

Jews wanted to stone Him for telling the truth. Jesus existed before Abraham. A lot of people don't

CHAPTER 1: GOD REVEALS HIMSELF

know this. They think Christmas was the start of Jesus. I have taught in churches where people looked astonished when I told them Jesus existed long before the Holy Ghost conceived Him in the womb of Mary. Jesus always has been and always shall be. He is eternal life personified. Beginning or end, if we go in either direction forever, we still never reach the beginning or the end. That is eternal. So it is with Jesus. He had no beginning and has no end. (We gain eternal life when we are saved. God turns us from everlasting past to everlasting future.) In the beginning, God was already there. God had already decided things and planned things. In the beginning, God created the world. That is where the Bible starts. The Bible doesn't start where God started because God had no beginning.

We need to understand several things:

I. The **pre-existence** of God--God existed before the time when we normally "begin."

II. The **incarnation** of God--Jesus is God manifest in the flesh. He came born of a woman and born of a virgin.

III. The **nature** of God--The Lord Jesus Christ is God and reveals God's nature.

I John 3:2 says,

"Beloved, now are we the sons of God, and it doth not yet appear what we shall be: But we know that, when he shall appear, we shall be like him; for we shall see him as he is."

One day the heavens will open, and Jesus will return. When Jesus comes back for us, we are going to see like we have never seen and understand like we have never understood. We are going to become like Jesus. Oh what a day that will be!

"Looking for that blessed hope, and the glorious appearing of the great God and our Saviour Jesus Christ" (Titus 2:13).

This hope of Christ's return enables us to live and endure in this wicked world. We have a God that is revealing certain things about Himself to us now. Further revelations will come in the future. I am looking forward to knowing more and more about God. We sing, **"More, about Jesus would I know."** We need also to long to know more and more about Who the true God is.

I John 2:27, 28 reads,

CHAPTER 1: GOD REVEALS HIMSELF

> *"But the anointing which ye have received of him abideth in you, and ye need not that any man teach you: but as the same anointing teacheth you of all things, and is truth, and is no lie, and even as it hath taught you, ye shall abide in him. And now, little children, abide in him; that, when he shall appear, we may have confidence, and not be ashamed before him at his coming."*

We have the indwelling Holy Spirit to teach us. As we think of the wonders of the return of Jesus, The Holy Spirit is teaching us about a Godhead. He is correcting our misunderstandings and pointing out truths and realities. He is teaching us one thing after another. The Bible says He teaches us **ALL** things. He is the teacher that never leaves anything out. We have Him within that we might know God.

> *"...This is life eternal, that they might know thee the only true God..."* (John 17:3).

What a wonderful thing it is that God wants to reveal Himself to us! He is not a distant God like the deist Thomas Jefferson believed. One who created everything and just let his creation run on and on. He is not a mysterious God that can't be known like the heathen and the Muslims believe. He is a God Who reveals Himself to us step by step. He has purposed that we know Him as the true God.

I John 4:9, 14 say,

> *"In this was manifested the love of God towards us, because that God sent his only begotten Son into the world, that we might live through him. And we have seen and do testify that the Father sent the Son to be the Saviour of the world."*

Because the Father loves us, He sent His own Son Jesus from Heaven to the world as a gift. Start there and consider how God reveals Himself to mankind.

CHAPTER 2
GOD IS TRIUNE

God is three, and God is one. This second point is found in **I John 5:7** where it says,

> *"For there are three that bear record in heaven, the Father, the Word, and the Holy Ghost: and these three are one."*

God is a tri-unity; we use the term Trinity. He is three that is one. We may say that we can't understand this. Wonderful! God is bigger than our intelligence. We would hate to have a God Who is as small as our own understanding. If we understood everything about God, we could just disregard Him. Instead, in reverence, we must bow and worship Him. Though God reveals Himself and we can know Him, there is a lot we do not understand.

He is a Triune God--God the Father, God the Son, and God the Holy Spirit. These three are One. We **don't have three gods, but neither are we Unitarians or Apostolics or Mormons with only one member in the godhead. We are not Hindus with many gods. We are**

not Muslims that only have an Allah. We are worshipping the true God.

I know **I John 5:7** is one of the most hated verses in the entire Bible. I have a friend that took this as his favorite verse. When asked why he chose this one, he said that the devil hates it more than any other verse; so he figured he would make it his favorite. Not a bad piece of logic. A lot of people have attacked this verse. The devil doesn't like it because it helps us get to know Who the **TRUE** God is.

Three are one. How does that work? **I John** tells us. Three examples in I John paint the working of the trinity.

I John 3:21, 23-24 states,

> *"Beloved, if our heart condemn us not, then have we confidence toward God. And this is his commandment, That we should believe on the name of his Son Jesus Christ, and love one another, as he gave us commandment. And he that keepeth his commandments dwelleth in him, and he in him. And hereby we know that he abideth in us, by the Spirit which he hath given us."*

CHAPTER 2: GOD IS TRIUNE

Each member of the Triune God (identified in **I John 5:7**) is shown here in one passage. We can study the passage or show it to someone else.

I John 4:2 says,

"Hereby know ye the Spirit of God: Every spirit that confesseth that Jesus Christ is come in the flesh is of God."

How do we know whether we have the Holy Spirit from God the Father or an evil spirit? We know by what is confessed about the Lord Jesus Christ--the second member of the Trinity. The Holy Spirit from God the Father will confess that Jesus Christ the Son is come in the flesh. Each has His distinct position—Father, Son, or Holy Spirit. Yet, they are one. That is unity.

A third example is found in **I John 4:13-15** where it reads,

"Hereby know we that we dwell in him, and he in us, because he hath given us of his Spirit. And we have seen and do testify that the Father sent the Son to be the Saviour of the world. Whosoever shall confess that Jesus is the Son of God, God dwelleth in him, and he in God."

Here we can see the Trinity—Father, Son, and Spirit. Some may say that the Trinity is a figment of people's imagination; but no, it is the teaching of the Word of God. The Word of God is the revelation of the true God. Father, Son, and Spirit are the One True God. God operates as a Trinity and reveals Himself as a Trinity.

I John 1:3 reads,

"That which we have seen and heard declare we unto you, that ye also may have fellowship with us: and truly our fellowship is with the Father, and with His Son Jesus Christ."

If we have fellowship with the Father, we have fellowship with the Son. We are to have fellowship with both and not just one. What about the Holy Spirit? Was He left out? He is indwelling us. As we fellowship with the Spirit inside us, we can fellowship with the Father and the Son. Three are one. God makes this very simple and understandable. Read **I John**, for it identifies the true God and His distinguishing marks.

I John 1:7b says,

CHAPTER 2: GOD IS TRIUNE

> *"...we have fellowship one with another, and the blood of Jesus Christ his Son cleanseth us from all sin."*

We must acknowledge both Father and Son unlike those that deny the unity of the two and the reality of both.

I John 2:23, 24 say,

> *"Whosoever denieth the Son, the same hath not the Father: (but) he that acknowledgeth the Son hath the Father also. Let that therefore abide in you, which ye have heard from the beginning. If that which ye have heard from the beginning shall remain in you, ye shall also continue in the Son, and in the Father."*

A distinction exists between Father and Son. Father, Son, and Spirit are One; but they are separate. There is a relationship. We need to grasp this because people will just lump Father, Son, and Spirit together like a lump of clay. *"This is God,"* they say and put that lump on a shelf. Those people may have done this intellectually rather than literally, but to do so really is a form of idolatry. They don't bother to find out and don't understand Who the true God is or how He operates.

I John 5:20 says,

> *"And we know that the Son of God is come, and hath given us an understanding, that we may know him that is true, and we are in him that is true, even in his Son Jesus Christ. This is the true God, and eternal life."*

Again, we see the Father-Son relationship. Both Father and Son are spoken of as being God.

I John 1:2 says,

> *"For the life was manifested, and we have seen it, and bear witness, and shew unto you that eternal life, which was with the Father, and was manifested unto us."*

We see that Jesus was with the Father. We also see that He has been sent of the Father.

I John 2:1 reads,

CHAPTER 2: GOD IS TRIUNE

"My little children, these things write I unto you, that ye sin not. And if any man sin, we have an advocate with the Father, Jesus Christ the righteous."

When we sin, our sins can be dealt with because Jesus the Son becomes our legal lawyer or advocate. He stands as our representative before God the Father. There is a distinction between Son and Father, but they work together on our behalf. They must do this in order to fully satisfy Divine justice and deal with the nature and the decrees of God.

I John 3:16 states,

"Hereby perceive we the love of God, because he laid down his life for us: and we ought to lay down our lives for the brethren."

God loves us and laid down His life. Neither the Holy Spirit nor the Father died for us, but Jesus did. He is called God. Jesus is God--absolutely God and fully God. He is the true God. He is not a lesser God, an angel, or a brother to the devil. He is not some good person or great teacher. He is God. This fact doesn't subtract anything from the Father or the Holy Spirit. Together these three are one God. Jesus loved us, died for us, and made it possible for us to have victory in our souls.

I John 5:5 says,

> *"Who is he that overcometh the world, but he that believeth that Jesus is the Son of God?"*

How do we have victory over the world? We believe that God sent His Son and that Jesus is the Son of God. We believe and trust in God Who reveals Himself as a Triune God with all three members working on our behalf. We don't have to get caught up in the world or become like the world because God is the opposite of the world. We can have victory over the world. Many people are stumbling and struggling because they have never truly understood Who the true God is.

I John 4:10 says,

> *"Herein is love, not that we loved God, but that he loved us, and sent his Son to be the propitiation for our sins."*

God loves us and sent His Son so our sins could be forgiven. We ourselves cannot atone for our sin. Purgatory does not exist. Our sins will not be burned up like the Seventh Day Adventists believe. However, God sent His Son--the only possible way for our sins to be forgiven. His Son came to be the propitiation for our sins.

I John 5:9-11 reads,

"If we receive the witness of men, the witness of God is greater: for this is the witness of God which he hath testified of his Son. He that believeth on the Son of God hath the witness in himself, he that believeth not God hath made him a liar; because he believeth not the record that God gave of his Son. And this is the record, that God hath given to us eternal life, and this life is in his Son."

The two themes in the book of I John--the true God and eternal life—are **wrapped together so tightly that we can't separate them. The Father sent the Son to be the propitiation for your sins and mine that we might have life. There is no eternal life apart from the Son. The Father sent Him; and the Holy Spirit makes Him real to us.**

Most people only exist. They are born and make it through year after year, but they have no sense of purpose or goal or preparation for eternity. They don't even want to think long range except maybe through a window of a few days, weeks, months, or years. However, for those who have eternal life, death is a door by which we joyfully enter into the presence of the true God and into greater revelation and knowledge and into the greater benefits of eternal life.

God reveals Himself. God is a Triune God. God is One. This is the true God. Any other that is called god is not the true God. We need to stand clearly on these truths. We need to be able to explain them because we will be running into more and more people who don't know them. They won't teach them in school anymore; and in most cases, they won't teach them in Sunday School. We will have neighbors, relatives, and fellow workers that don't know Who the true God is.

One hot day back in the late 60's or early 70's, I was in a little community in Ohio. I had spoken at a Memorial Day service and had a chance to tell how Jesus died to give us His life. An elderly officer in the Methodist church that had been a principal of their school came up to me. He told me that we all worship the same god, and we all go to the same place. I tried to be kind because we are not to rebuke an elder. I answered, *"That is what scares me."* Most people do worship the same god—a false god. They are, in fact, all headed to the same place. We are going to hear this same mantra over and over. If we are not careful, we will become tolerant; and toleration will eventually turn into acceptance. We must know and be able to clearly declare Who the true God is.

CHAPTER 3

GOD IS HOLY

I John 2:20 says,

> *"But ye have an unction from the Holy One, and ye know all things."*

God calls Himself the Holy One. He is a Holy God. He has never sinned and is not going to sin. He is not going to lie or cooperate with a lie. He is not going to assist in or have any part of anything unholy. There is so much that is unholy that goes on in the name of religion, and people ask God's blessing. They forget that God is the Holy One. He is Holy by His very nature.

In **Isaiah 6:3b** we have a picture with the beings around the throne of God crying,

> *"Holy, holy, holy, is the LORD of Hosts…."*

In **Revelation 4:8b** we find a scene in heaven of the creatures around the throne crying,

> *"…Holy, holy, holy, LORD God Almighty, which was, and is, and is to come."*

Our God is a thrice-holy God. Each member of the Triune God is holy. God is fully and completely holy.

According to the Bible, the holiness of God is a truth proclaimed in heaven. However, God's holiness is one of the least proclaimed truths in the churches of America.

Now, having said that, we need to identify what the Bible means when it says God is holy. I John defines His Holiness.

I John 2:27 says,

"But the anointing which ye have received of him abideth in you, and ye need not that any man teach you: but as the same anointing teacheth you of all things, and is truth, and is no lie...."

Holiness is truth and is no lie. Holiness won't make room for lying, but instead demands absolute truth. God by nature is Truth. He is Love, but He is Truth, too. God is Holy.

I John 4:5,6 states,

"They are of the world: therefore speak they of the world, and the world

CHAPTER 3: GOD IS HOLY

heareth them. We are of God: he that knoweth God heareth us; he that is not of God heareth not us. Hereby know we the spirit of truth, and the spirit of error."

We wonder why some people don't listen to truth. It is because they don't know God. They listen to the world because they are of the world. We can know the spirit of truth and the spirit of error by their audience—those who hear them. It would scare me to have the ear of the world.

Whenever the world approves of a church, it is probably no longer a church. The world hears its own. God's people hear their own. That is how the spirit of truth and the spirit of error are separated. If we look at a man's audience, we can tell something about him. We may not immediately discern his exact problem; but if the crowd is wrong, we can be sure there is a problem with the man. If a church has the audience of the world, we can be sure there is something wrong with that church. If a religious group or periodical has the ear of the world, we can be sure that something is wrong. The world hears the spirit of error. The spirit of truth is tuned into by those that know the holy God. The world wants a god who will favor something less than holiness. They think that God will approve of them and accept them.

I hadn't been pastor at a certain church long before one of the leading young women who had grown up in the church came and told me that she wanted to divorce her husband and marry another man. She explained why this was more satisfactory to her. I told her that this wasn't acceptable to God, the Bible, or her new pastor. She argued that the Scriptures say that God moves in strange and mysterious ways His wonders to perform! I quickly told her that wasn't in the Bible, but rather in a poem written by a lost man. She was shaken. She thought God would approve of her immoral desires. She had the wrong god.

I have met many people whose god is not the God of the Bible. The God of the Bible is a holy God--a truthful God that won't have any part of lies or that which is wrong. Because He is holy, God can't bless just anything we may want blessed. We have to know God and His nature.

I John 5:6 reads,

"This is he that came by water and blood, even Jesus Christ; not by water only, but by water and blood. And it is the

Spirit that beareth witness, because the Spirit is truth."

John is defining holiness. When you know God is holy and that involves His being Truth, then you will know that He won't have any part with un-truth. If you want to twist the truth, God won't back you. I have heard it told that if you tell a lie to get someone saved, God will bless that because love will cover a multitude of sins. We have men's opinions thrown at us; but if we know the nature of God, we will know they are incorrect opinions. God is Holy and God is Truth. He is not going to have any part with lies.

I John 5:9 says,

"If we receive the witness of men, the witness of God is greater: for this is the witness of God which he hath testified of His Son."

Notice that the witness of God is greater than the witness of man. A man can tell the truth "to the best of his ability" or "to the best of his knowledge." However, when God speaks, His ability and knowledge are unlimited. No crack enables us to twist, turn, or re-interpret what He said. When God speaks, man has no room to say, *"That is just His viewpoint. From another viewpoint it might look a little different."* The witness of God is greater than the witness of the most honest, truth-telling man that ever lived. God's witness is greater, because God is fully holy.

Christians are holy in position but should desire to become more and more holy in practice. I believe it was Robert Murray McCheyne who prayed, *"God make me as holy as you can make a saved sinner."* That is what we need. We need to become more and more holy. If we are going to have any evidence or power of holiness in our lives, we need to guard what we say. In **Acts chapter 3**, the people came to ask Peter about the healing of a lame man. Peter told them not to look at himself and John as if it were by their power of holiness that this man was healed.

> *"Ye men of Israel, why marvel ye at this? Or why look ye so earnestly on us, as though by our own power or holiness we had made this man to walk? The God of Abraham, and of Isaac, and of Jacob, the God of our fathers, hath glorified his Son Jesus...."*

In those days, they recognized the power of holiness and a holy life. We used to recognize that power in America. Some people were so holy that they had spiritual power or a moral force. We have so few holy people today that we don't see that holiness produces power. Lack of holiness will rob us of any moral authority.

Truthfulness is a necessity. If we twist the truth once, people will doubt us for a long time. They have a right to. But God is fully truthful, and His witness is far greater than man's.

I John 1:5-7, says,

> *"This then is the message which we have heard of him, and declare unto you, that God is light, and in him is no darkness at all. If we say that we have fellowship with him, and walk in darkness, we lie, and do not the truth: But if we walk in the light, as he is in the light, we have fellowship one with another, and the blood of Jesus Christ his Son cleanseth us from all sin."*

God is light and walks in light. There is no darkness in God. He doesn't have anything to do with darkness. People that must hide their acts and thoughts are not walking in step with God. God is holy, and being holy requires light. To walk with Him in His holiness means we have to walk in light. He will not even fellowship with us if we get into any darkness. We lose His fellowship. We can claim we have it. Many people do; but if they are walking in darkness, God says they are liars. We have to leave the darkness to get into the light where God is. He is holy, and He dwells in light. There and there alone will He fellowship with us. This is the God of the Bible.

I grow weary of people telling me that they are close to God and fellowshipping with Him, yet something remains in their life that is not light and truth but darkness and lies. They disregard the very nature of God. We must know the true God so that we can be **"strong and do exploits"** according to **Daniel 11:32**.

I John 2:8 reads,

"Again, a new commandment I write unto you, which thing is true in him and in you: because the darkness is past, and the true light now shineth."

This speaks of someone who left the darkness for the light. He put the darkness behind him because God is not going to fellowship with those who walk in

CHAPTER 3: GOD IS HOLY

darkness. God is holy. We must leave the darkness and go to the light where God dwells.

I John 2:9 continues,

> *"He that saith he is in the light, and hateth his brother, is in darkness even until now."*

We may ask if a Christian can reach the point of hating his brother. Bitterness can stir things up in us that we don't even want to consider. We will find ourselves in such darkness, such loss of fellowship, and such frustration that we wonder if we ever did know God. How is it that God left us? He didn't. We left Him. He is holy, and He won't fellowship with us when we are involved in sin. The implication is that we must get out of our darkness.

I John 2:29 states,

> *"If ye know that he is righteous, ye know that every one that doeth righteousness is born of him."*

He is righteous. **"Righteous"** is not the absence of sin, but rather is something that is to be done-- **"doeth righteousness."**

For some, holiness is to *not* do this or that. Certain things we should not do, of course. We don't want to be a partaker in darkness. Light is a part of the definition of holiness. Truth is part of that definition too. We can't just be neutral and *not* say anything. We must speak truth. Again, righteousness is something that we do.

Let's use a cup of water as an example. As far as I know, that cup never danced, drank liquor, smoked, dressed immodestly, cursed, took drugs, or got into immorality. So, is it a holy cup? Some people define holy by a whole list of "don'ts." A potato would be holy by their definition. By God's definition, holiness is not only what we don't do and what we left behind but also what we are going to do. We are going to do that which is righteous. God always does that which is right. Holiness demands doing right or acting out your righteousness. I know there is positional righteousness, but everything positional is revealed to us so that we have the foundation for practice. Position without practice is emptiness.

What have we been doing right? Have we stopped doing wrong and started doing right? God never had to change because He never did wrong and

CHAPTER 3: GOD IS HOLY

never will. He has always done right. Wasn't that the basis of Abraham's praying for Sodom and Gomorrah?

"...Shall not the Judge of all the earth do right?" (Genesis 18:25b).

Abraham knew about the righteousness of God. He was basing his request on God's holiness. Holiness requires doing what is right! God will always do what is right. He will do right for those saved and for those lost. It would be a terrible thing to put lost people in heaven. They wouldn't fit, not because of a space problem, but because of a nature problem. Often, in their hearts, people are secret enemies against the strictness of God. They don't like His holiness. They would be willing to struggle and be a little better, but they don't want to be **THAT** holy or **THAT** much like God. They don't want a God that is holy and demands the same of them. He said, "...***Be ye holy; for I am holy***" **(I Peter 1:16).** God has a place prepared for those that have lived without Him all of their lives. It is a place without the God of glory.

I John 1:8, 10 read,

"If we say that we have no sin, we deceive ourselves, and the truth is not in us. If we say that we have not sinned, we

make him a liar, and his word is not in us."

Involved in His holiness is the fact that God is actively against sin. He is in opposition to it, and He exposes it. Holiness requires exposing sin. We will not be holy until we repent and confess our sins. If we won't expose them, we cover them; and

"He that covereth his sins shall not prosper..." (Prov. 28:13a).

That is what the Bible teaches. It is the nature of God in holiness to deal with sin. He is never in favor of it but is always against it. People don't want that kind of a God. They want a God that will overlook their sin, one who might even encourage them a little, or one who will at least let them feel comfortable in sin. They are not sure they want the truth. They don't always want to do what is right. We begin to wonder what they do want in their God. In our churches, when it comes to the matter of holiness and His nature, do we have the true God?

I John 3:5 says,

CHAPTER 3: GOD IS HOLY

> *"And ye know that he was manifested to take away our sins; and in him is no sin."*

Jesus

> *"...was in all points tempted like as we are, yet without sin" (Heb. 4:15b).*

Jesus is holy.

There is no sin that has ever been or will ever be in God. This is part of His holiness. God will not allow sin in Himself.

I John 3:2, 3 says,

> *"Beloved, now are we the sons of God, and it doth not yet appear what we shall be: but we know that, when he shall appear, we shall be like him: for we shall see him as he is. And every man that hath this hope in him purifieth himself, even as he is pure."*

When we meet God, we are going to see Him in His holiness. He is so pure that His purity will move us to purify ourselves in expectation of seeing Him.

I remember knocking at a door. My wife was waiting in the car. I had told her that if something went wrong, she was to drive away and get help. A woman whom I had seldom seen came to the door. She immediately started to tremble and began to say, *"It is not me. It is not my fault. I am not responsible for what is going on in my house."* I told her to just inform two people that I was there and wanted to see them. She told them but returned saying that they didn't want to talk to me. Why do you suppose that they didn't want to talk to their pastor? It was a man and a woman who weren't husband and wife. They hadn't expected me to show up and weren't prepared to speak to me.

I wonder. When Jesus comes back, will people be prepared to face the true God Who is absolutely pure and holy? If a pastor appearing on a porch makes someone tremble, what do you think it will be like when Jesus appears? Jesus--Who is absolutely holy--is coming back. Those that have this hope will be purifying themselves. They won't be shocked when He returns and they stand in His presence. We have a holy God. We won't want to live sinfully when we realize how holy He is.

I John 3:6 says,

CHAPTER 3: GOD IS HOLY

> *"Whosoever abideth in him sinneth not: whosoever sinneth hath not seen him, neither known him."*

A holy God will not have any part with sin. People who live in sin don't know Him. They may talk, preach, teach, or sing like they know God; but they don't.

I John 3:9, 10 says,

> *"Whosoever is born of God doth not commit sin; for his seed remaineth in him: and he cannot sin, because he is born of God. In this the children of God are manifest, and the children of the devil: whosoever doeth not righteousness is not of God, neither he that loveth not his brother."*

God is such a holy God that when He saves us, He stops our sin life. While we may try at times, we can never pick sin up and run with it again. You may say that you know people that God saved out of some particular sin, and they went back to it. I know some people who <u>thought</u> they got saved out of a sin and went back to it. **II Peter 2:22b** is a Scripture for that.

> *"...The dog is turned to his own vomit again; and the sow that was washed to her wallowing in the mire."*

By what the Bible says here, we can tell the difference between a saved person and a lost one. A Holy God will work some holiness into a saved person's soul. When God convicts, it is not just the guilt of his sin that makes the sin look so awful to a sinner. It is the absence of holiness and the sinner's desire for holiness. I have known people to weep over having stolen a couple of flowers or stamps. We may think stealing a few stamps or flowers isn't a big thing; but those sins brought the individuals short of holiness. That broke their hearts. It wasn't the big thing they had done, but rather the big thing they had missed. Do you understand what I am saying? We think that if a person has a big enough stack of sins, he ought to weep and be sorry. No, the lack of holiness is the thing that ought to break his heart. No matter how small the matter-- taking advantage of the system, shaving a few pennies here or there, miswriting time on a time card, saying that the boss really did owe that time to us--God is watching us all the time; and He is holy.

I John 5:16 reads,

CHAPTER 3: GOD IS HOLY

"If any man see his brother sin a sin which is not unto death, he shall ask, and he shall give him life for them that sin not unto death. There is a sin unto death: I do not say that he shall pray for it."

This verse is talking about praying for a saved brother who is sinning. Pray for him that he will be recovered and stop his sinning because God is a holy God. God will not let His children disgrace His name. He is severe when it comes to sin in the life of a believer. God is not going to let him continue committing sin on a constant basis. If a believer keeps on in that sin, he is going to die because God is not going to let His children go on and on in sin. We need to know what the sins unto death are. Prayerfully consider **Romans 8:11-14; I Corinthians 6:9-11; Galatians 5:19-21; Ephesians 5:1-8; and Revelation 21:8.**

I John 4:17 says,

"Herein is our love made perfect, that we may have boldness in the day of judgment: because as he is, so are we in this world."

God is holy, and we ought to be also. A day of judgment is coming, and we don't want to be disgraced. I have been to the cemetery for people who have died because of an absence of holiness and because of misplaced values. In most cases, they had committed no great sin in the eyes of the world or even in the eyes of the church, but they had violated God's laws. God judged them and took them. They might not have discerned the Lord's body.

> *"For this cause many are weak, and sickly among you, and many sleep" (I Cor. 11:29c–30).*

Knowing God is holy must affect how we think, choose, and live. I would like to face judgment with a God-honoring trail behind me.

I John 5:18 says,

> *"We know that whosoever is born of God sinneth not; but he that is begotten of God keepeth himself, and that wicked one toucheth him not."*

God is not going to let the devil have His child. He will take His child home. I have heard people say, *"God saved him thirty years ago, and he has lived out in the world. He's a backslidden, carnal Christian."* For a while, this person may have acted like he was saved;

CHAPTER 3: GOD IS HOLY

but I would like to suggest that he never was. God is a holy God; and as a holy God, He cannot tolerate sin. He is against it, exposes it, and deals with it. This is the true God. Any other god is the desire of man's corrupted heart and a god of man's imagination. Man desires to transform the true God of the Bible until they have made Him into a modified Santa Claus. We need the true God.

WHO IS THE TRUE GOD?

CHAPTER 4

GOD IS LOVE

I John 2:5 reads,

> *"But whoso keepeth his word in him verily is the love of God perfected...."*

The love of God is not in everybody? It doesn't grow in everybody? No, the love of God is perfected in those that keep His Word. To some people, the idea that God is love means that everyone is going to heaven. Origen (186-253 A.D.) of Alexandria, Egypt, believed that everyone, including the devil, was going to heaven because God was love. He believed the planets, sun, moon, and stars had souls and were going to heaven because God was a loving God. The love of God is perfected, however, only in the hearts of those that keep His Word. That truth could be rather frightening to the people that believe that God loves enough to just let them go to heaven. Let's consider the ones that do have the love of God within and will be taken to heaven. Do we qualify?

I John 2:15 says,

> *"Love not the world, neither the things that are in the world. If any man*

love the world, the love of the Father is not in him."

Those that love the world don't have God's love in them. The true God will not put His love in those who love the world.

I John 3:1 reads,

"Behold, what manner of love the Father hath bestowed upon us, that we should be called the sons of God: therefore the world knoweth us not, because it knew him not."

God does not operate by the world's manner of love but rather by His own. The world didn't know Him, and the world doesn't know His people. His people are the ones with God's manner of love. His people aren't of the world. God bestows His love; His love is not an automatic right for all human beings. That contradicts much of the teaching in evangelical, charismatic, and liberal circles. I guarantee that we wouldn't have to look far to find someone who is of the world yet thinks they are going to heaven because God loves them.

I John 3:16 says,

CHAPTER 4: GOD IS LOVE

> *"Hereby, perceive we the love of God, because he laid down his life for us: and we ought to lay down our lives for the brethren."*

God's love requires us to sacrifice, suffer, and die if need be.

We may say that we have the love of God. What are we doing for brothers and sisters who are suffering? Some among the saved widows (our sisters) in the country of Georgia must live on $5 a month. That won't even buy a pair of shoes in America. Is the love of God in us? Instead, do we have the love of the world and its fashion, approval, and comforts? What are we doing for missions? There are souls we need to reach. Do we just drop a few nickels in the offering once in a while? Are we willing, instead, to lay down our lives? Some people talk about the love of God, but the love they demonstrate doesn't look like God's love. I wonder what kind of love they actually possess.

I John 3:17 reads,

> *"But whoso hath this world's good, and seeth his brother have need, and shutteth up his bowels of compassion*

from him, how dwelleth the love of God in him?"

If another's need doesn't stir us and move us to action, what makes us think that we have the love of God in us? We used to use clichés like *"To be Christian is to be missionary."* Why? Our bowels of compassion were stirred for those who didn't have the Light we had. Today, those without compassion say, *"We have God's love. We don't have to care about others."* I just ask them what the Bible asks. How dwelleth the love of God in you?

What kind of love do we have if it doesn't match the true God's manner of love? What kind of god gives us a cozy, warm feeling but lets us live cold-heartedly toward the needs of saved people and lost people throughout the world? That god is not the God of the Bible! That god is not the true God! The true God's love is going to make us missionary-minded. His love will make us compassionate particularly towards those that are saved and in need. His love will stir us to action.

Years ago I read about the missionary speaker and writer, Ord Morrow. He went to a Bible conference and had an opportunity to meet a man whom he had wanted to meet. Mr. Morrow asked this man if he was

CHAPTER 4: GOD IS LOVE

going to be speaking on missions anytime that week. The man replied, *"Oh no, I am the Bible teacher. You are the missions speaker. You handle missions, and I will teach the Bible."* Did this man think that missions wasn't in the Bible? Who is this god that doesn't stir our hearts? The true God will put a zeal and burning fire in us.

I John 4:7-12 reads,

"Beloved, let us love one another: for love is of God; and every one that loveth is born of God, and knoweth God. He that loveth not knoweth not God; for God is love. In this was manifested the love of God toward us, because that God sent his only begotten Son into the world, that we might live through him. Herein is love, not that we loved God, but that he loved us, and sent his Son to be the propitiation for our sins. Beloved, if God so loved us, we ought also to love one another. No man hath seen God at any time. If we love one another, God dwelleth in us, and his love is perfected in us."

God didn't give us His love to make us selfish but to make us pro-active. He wants us to get busy and reach out to others.

I John dealt with errors then that we still face today. God is love, but be careful to know the Biblical definition of love. We have allowed the liberals to redefine Bible terminology. Let the Bible define Bible terminology. **I John 4:19** states,

"We love him, because he first loved us."

God's love isn't a warm, comfortable feeling. His love produces something. God expects us to respond with a similar love. We will do something. God is love. This is the true God.

CHAPTER 5

GOD IS MIGHTY

I John 1:7-2:2 says

"But if we walk in the light, as he is in the light, we have fellowship one with another, and the blood of Jesus Christ his Son cleanseth us from all sin. If we say that we have no sin, we deceive ourselves, and the truth is not in us. If we confess our sins, he is faithful and just to forgive us our sins, and to cleanse us from all unrighteousness. If we say that we have not sinned, we make him a liar, and his word is not in us. My little children, these things write I unto you, that ye sin not. And if any man sin, we have an advocate with the Father, Jesus Christ the righteous: And he is the propitiation for our sins: and not for ours only, but also for the sins of the whole world."

God is a mighty God. He can deal with sin. He can forgive sin and cleanse from sin. He can deliver from sin. The government cannot do that. Neither scientists nor doctors can do it. Neither education nor money can do it. However, the almighty God is able to take our sins, forgive our sins, and cleanse us from them. He is the great and mighty God. He is the sovereign God. The devil can't keep Him from taking our sins away. Think of the load He lifted from us. If that load has never been lifted from you, you need the God Who can lift it. You can struggle, reform, change, study, pray, sing, and weep; but it takes God to get rid of your sins. Recognize God's great might and power. Let the mighty God work in your soul.

In **chapter 2:12b** it says He forgives us for "***His name's sake.***" **Chapter 3:5** says He will "***take away our sins.***" I am so glad that God helped me deal with some of the sins with which I once struggled. God did surgery, cut those sins out, and took them away. I don't have the struggles I once had. I know I still have a sin nature. You have one too.

However, isn't it good to know that the sins of the past can no longer haunt us? We shouldn't be satisfied just to be forgiven for a past act. We should want God to purge that sin. Our mighty God can take it away.

I had my appendix removed in Greenville, SC. The appendix was in pieces, and they took all the

CHAPTER 5: GOD IS MIGHTY

pieces they could find. I hope they found them all. I would hate for them to have gone after my appendix and have found some pieces but not all. We need spiritual surgery from time to time to have something cut out of our life. God is the surgeon big enough to do that. No one but our great God can deal with sin.

I John 3:22 says,

"And whatsoever we ask, we receive of him, because we keep his commandments, and do those things that are pleasing in his sight."

The God of the Bible hears and answers prayer. Allah can't do that. The god of most people can't. People often pray like they flip a coin. They hope the prayer lands heads up, and they get something. If they can get more people to throw prayers up, something is more likely to happen down here. They think. They don't know the God Who is almighty, has all power, and can do as He wills.

When it comes to our praying, how great and powerful is our God? How big is our God? How much does He have? How much—in nickels, dimes, quarters, dollars--can we ask from Him? Some people pray in a way that makes us think that their god is bankrupt, helpless, and deaf. We wonder why they even try to pray. They end up quitting. How much can we get from God in prayer? George Mueller gave us an example of what can be done. Hudson Taylor, Adoniram Judson, William Carey, Charles Spurgeon, Dwight Moody, and many others did also.

The problem is not the source or supply but the channel. How much can God funnel through us? Most of us are a funnel that is only about one thirty-second of an inch wide. We may try to grow a little spiritually and get up to one sixteenth of an inch wide. However, when God funnels His answer down, He wants us four or five inches wide so that He can pour His answer right on through.

I John 5:14, 15 says,

> *"And this is the confidence that we have in him, that, if we ask anything according to his will, he heareth us: And if we know that he hear us, whatsoever we ask, we know that we have the petitions that we desired of him."*

These verses tell us that we can be certain that the answer is coming and prepare accordingly.

CHAPTER 5: GOD IS MIGHTY

The first time I heard about Brother Bob Doom was through a student that had heard him preach. Brother Bob had caused a lot of controversy because he had preached on the Lordship of Christ. The student called me to say someone had preached on this and believed the same gospel and the same Bible we did. I was told Brother Bob was the son-in-law of James Stewart, of whom I had heard. When I asked how I could get in touch with Brother Bob, I was told he was returning to Scotland but would be coming back to the United States. I tried to schedule him for a meeting. Those I talked to weren't able to schedule anything because they didn't know what he had already scheduled. I called them back later and asked them to tell Brother Bob that we would like to have him on certain dates. Then I announced to the church that, God willing, we were having a preacher coming from Scotland and told them his name and other details. I had prayed, and I was satisfied. It was settled in my heart, and I was certain that it was going to happen. Though previously I had never met Brother Bob, we have now been close friends for nearly thirty years.

Our God is so great that He can give us certainty of the answer before it arrives. If He did this for me, He can do it for you. It is not that I am great, but God is. We have the same Saviour, the same salvation, the same Book, the same promises, and the same great God!

I have been able to go into places of danger and be satisfied that I would return. God had convinced me that I needed to do certain things when I got back, so how could they kill me while I was there? What if they had tried? God could have handled that. Maybe they did try? I don't know. Don't tempt God and play at this sort of thing. I am just saying that God is big enough, and we can rise above worrying about circumstances. We sometimes think of God's greatness only in salvation. He is great in His living for us. God is great in how we live once we are saved. We need to grasp this and live accordingly. Sometimes we talk like our God is great, but we live like He is weak.

I John 2:6 says,

"He that saith he abideth in him ought himself also so to walk, even as he walked."

Here God makes it clear that He empowers us to live a holy life. In **verses 20 and 27** of the same chapter, we are told that He teaches us **ALL** things. God is so great that there is nothing He can't teach us. From the Word of God, we learn anything that we need to learn.

CHAPTER 5: GOD IS MIGHTY

Some may learn faster and some slower. However, if we are saved, our learning ability is changed because we have a great God to teach us.

I John 3:2 says,

> *"Beloved, now are we the sons of God, and it doeth not yet appear what we shall be: but we know that, when he shall appear, we shall be like him; for we shall see him as he is."*

God is going to make us like Jesus one day. Imagine, making me like Jesus! That will require a great God. Won't it? Will it require a great God to make the final adjustments that make you like Jesus? When we see Him, a great God will make us like Him in heart, soul, and desire.

> *"For if our heart condemn us, God is greater than our heart…" (I John 3:20a). "If man has a witness, he is greater than man and his witness is greater" (I John 5:9).*

God is greater than my heart, greater than man, and greater than all. I love this great God we have.

I John 3:8-10 says,

> *"He that committeth sin is of the devil; for the devil sinneth from the beginning. For this purpose the Son of God was manifested, that he might destroy the works of the devil. Whosoever is born of God doth not commit sin; for his seed remaineth in him: and he cannot sin, because he is born of God. In this the children of God are manifest, and the children of the devil: whosoever doeth not righteousness is not of God, neither he that loveth not his brother."*

He is so great that God can defeat the devil himself and destroy whatever the devil may accomplish.

I John 3:12 says,

> *"Not as Cain, who was of that wicked one, and slew his brother. And wherefore slew he him? Because his own works were evil, and his brother's righteous."*

It looked like the devil had stopped the family line for the Messiah. However, God is greater than the devil. God is greater than all of the devil's people and

CHAPTER 5: GOD IS MIGHTY

all of their acts. God sent another son, Seth, and ran the family line through him. We have a God that overcomes whatever man may try to do and whatever the devil may plot. The conspiracies of the devil and man are nothing compared to our mighty God. Most assuredly, I believe in conspiracies. Even more so, I believe in a great God. I believe that the devil and his people would have fulfilled their conspiracies, but we have an almighty God. He has frustrated the conspirators again and again. The conspirators make their plan, set a deadline, and get everything in position. God puffs, and their plan is gone. I love to watch the working of our great God. Don't you? Some people fret when they see what the devil is trying to accomplish. They worry when they see what people are doing. If we could just see how great God is, we could confidently march on. This great God is the true God. He rules in the affairs of men.

I John 4:4 says,

"Ye are of God, little children, and have overcome them: because greater is he that is in you, than he that is in the world."

He is not only our God, but He is in us. I did something several years ago that would have been foolish if God hadn't directed me. I went with another man to visit a spiritist community of 10,000 people. Witches, warlocks, and demon-possessed people worshiped devils in a big temple. The worshipers behaved like charismatics. They marched around and gathered around us. When they were about to put hands on us, I just bowed my head and started praying. They pulled their hands back. I don't know if they were burnt or what happened. **Hebrews 12:29** says, *"For our God is a consuming fire."* Nearby, people were speaking in tongues, whooping and hollering, and raising their hands. Where we were, they couldn't do those things. It wasn't long until people near us started wandering off. Finally, I looked over at the fellow with me and asked if he had had enough. We both had, so we walked out. People there were glad.

Why did I do it?

"...Greater is he that is in you than he that is in the world" (I John 4:4b).

I wouldn't tempt the devil, but I believe God wanted me there. The people that took us didn't even

CHAPTER 5: GOD IS MIGHTY

want to follow us into the spiritist community. They stayed back and were waiting when we came out.

Do we really believe in the true God—the almighty, sovereign God? If we face a demon-possessed person or demon-possessed people, can we rest in the greatness of our God; or do we quiver in fear? God will handle anything as long as we are in His will. He is big enough.

I received a phone call from a drunken man who wanted to commit suicide. My son and I went to his home and found his wife outside and scared to go into the house. The man told me he would kill me if I came in. I told him I didn't think he would because I was coming in the name of Jesus. At times the gun was in his mouth. Sometimes it was pointed to his brain. Part of the time, the gun was pointed at my brain; and part of the time, it was pointed at my son's brain. For nearly two hours, we talked with him and witnessed to him and quoted Scripture. While one of us was talking, the other one was praying. How could I go into that home? I was not tempting God. We sometimes act like we don't really have a sovereign God. We need to act on the truth. We have a God greater than a drunken, demon-possessed, lost man with a gun in his hand. The true God is a mighty, mighty God.

I John 5:18 says,

> *"We know that whosoever is born of God sinneth not; but he that is begotten of God keepeth himself, and that wicked one toucheth him not."*

Because our God is so great, the devil cannot destroy us. Shadrach, Meshach, and Abednego were thrown into a furnace. The men who came near the opening of that furnace were burnt up; but Shadrach, Meshach, and Abednego could even walk around in the fire. They knew the true God, and He was there walking with them. Because they knew God, these three men could come out of that furnace past the corpses of those who had thrown them in.

Daniel was thrown into a den of lions, but the lions didn't touch him. When Daniel came out of that den, they threw others in. None of those others hit the bottom before every bone in their bodies was broken by those hungry lions. Daniel knew God. Joseph could do right and not fear the lies of Potiphar's wife. The prison keeper would respect him, and one day Pharaoh himself would need him. Joseph had a great God. David didn't fear Goliath because he had a great God.

CHAPTER 5: GOD IS MIGHTY

There are numerous other people in the Bible that can be cited. We know their secret. They knew the true God. That is the God of the Bible, and the God we need. The true God is the God about which we need to read in His Word, the God on which we need to meditate, and the God with which we need to saturate ourselves. We can then live in His light.

WHO IS THE TRUE GOD?

CHAPTER 6

GOD GIVES COMMANDS

Many people view God as the "man upstairs." He is a God to whom they can run when in trouble but whom they can ignore the rest of the time. That is not the God of the Bible. It is no wonder that those who have this warped view of God end up in the predicaments that they do. The God of the Bible gives commands AND expects them to be obeyed.

I John 2:3-11 says,

> *"And hereby we do know that we know him, if we keep his commandments. He that saith, I know him, and keepeth not his commandments, is a liar, and the truth is not in him. But whoso keepeth his word, in him verily is the love of God perfected: hereby know we that we are in him. He that saith he abideth in him ought himself also so to walk, even as he walked. Brethren, I write no new commandment unto you, but an old commandment which ye had from the beginning. The old commandment is the word which ye have heard from the*

beginning. Again, a new commandment I write unto you, which thing is true in him and in you: because the darkness is past, and the true light now shineth. He that saith he is in the light, and hateth his brother, is in darkness even until now. He that loveth his brother abideth in the light, and there is none occasion of stumbling in him. But he that hateth his brother is in darkness, and walketh in darkness, and knoweth not whither he goeth, because that darkness hath blinded his eyes."

God makes it clear that He has given us some commandments. They are already given and recorded. God is a God that gives commands, and saved people respond to those commands. Those that don't respond to His commands don't belong to Him.

With just a glance out into the congregation, I can catch my son's eye. I can gesture, and he will know exactly what I want. Each of my children at an early age knew what I meant when I motioned certain ways. When God gives commandments, His children tune in and obey. Those who are not His children stubbornly rebel. They reject His commandments and won't obey.

CHAPTER 6: GOD GIVES COMMANDS

We have a generation that rejects the commands of God and says that they don't have to obey. They aren't interested in His commands and don't want to obey them, yet they still claim that they belong to Him. They don't know God. He didn't give those commandments as options, suggestions, or recommendations. They are commandments. They carry force--the force of the almighty God Who stands behind them.

Isaiah 33:22 says,

"For the LORD is our judge, the LORD is our lawgiver, the LORD is our king, he will save us."

We will not find a simpler definition of the Lordship of Christ. The law God gave to His people is tied closely to salvation. God saved us so that we are able to be obedient. We keep the law because we are saved. God is present in our hearts, and He changes us. The Bible says that if a person doesn't keep God's commandments and yet says he knows God, he lies (**I John 2:4**). We are not saved by keeping the law. Lost people know God has given commands, and they can't keep them. That is why they grieve and mourn over their sins. Every time we lower the level of what God has commanded we create a comfort zone for lost people. They don't see how guilty, how incapable, and how helpless they are. They don't see how much they need God to save and change them so that they can keep His law. The law wasn't to save us but to show us our need of a Saviour.

We have an example of one of His commandments in **I John 3:23, 24** where it says,

> *"And this is his commandment, That we should believe on the name of his Son Jesus Christ, and love one another, as he gave us commandment. And he that keepeth his commandments dwelleth in him, and he in him. And hereby we know that he abideth in us, by the Spirit which he hath given us."*

Notice that obedience to commandments shows our relationship with God. The command is given to believe. Belief is not optional. Belief in the Lord Jesus Christ is not a suggestion but a command of Almighty God. People go to Hell because they won't keep His command. We are sinners by nature and practice. We are commanded to repent and believe the gospel, yet many refuse to obey. Men defy His command and

CHAPTER 6: GOD GIVES COMMANDS

don't believe. They think they can go on and not have to answer to God. We sometimes present God's commands as good ideas and hope someone will decide to try them. People need to be told that God's commands are, in fact, commands. Belief is God's command.

I John 5:2 says,

> *"By this we know that we love the children of God, when we love God, and keep his commandments."*

How do you know that you rightly love God's children? You rightly love God, and you keep His commandments. They go together.

We continue in **verse 3** of the same chapter,

> *"For this is the love of God, that we keep his commandments...."*

A lot of people talk about the love of God while they are breaking His commandments. They don't know the Bible or the God of the Bible.

The end of the same verse says,
"...And his commandments are not grievous."

When God saves a sinner, He makes us a new creature in Christ Jesus. What we struggled to do and failed becomes normal, natural, and acceptable to the new nature that God put in our hearts. His commandments are not grievous. People that struggle and say that God's commandments are so hard, are saying that they don't really belong to Him.

We enjoy a Commander that always tells us to do what is right. We know that He tells us what is necessary, and we know that in the end our obedience will work to our good. We might have to suffer a little now; but if we will suffer with Him, we will reign with Him.

"Yea, and all that will live godly in Christ Jesus shall suffer persecution" (II Tim. 3:12).

Suffering and glory go together. So if obedience to God's command means some suffering, we look ahead to the joy that is before us. It is not so grievous to suffer a little now when we consider what is coming later. When we know the true God, we don't find His commandments to be grievous. God is not trying to hurt us or make us miserable. His commandments are for our good.

CHAPTER 6: GOD GIVES COMMANDS

The Sabbath was created for man and not man for the Sabbath. The Lord's Day is one time we can justify a long afternoon nap! I know when I was only five or six years of age, Sunday naps didn't sound quite so great. I am beginning to understand more and more just how wonderful an opportunity like that can be. I am beginning to realize that we won't have anything to look forward to if we work all seven days in a week. It's wonderful when we have an opportunity to take a day off and just spend it resting, worshipping, and serving God. God didn't create the Sabbath to hurt us. He made it because we needed it. It is for our benefit.

God gave the command about not bearing false witness so that people can trust us and so that we can find others we can trust. That is a good thing. God also gave the command not to steal. It is good to know that some people are not going to rob us. We can trust them. Another of God's commands tells us not to commit adultery. We can trust our spouse. Isn't that a blessing?

The true God's commands are for our benefit. They help the lost see how sinful they are and help the saved be blessed. The saved still have the old sin nature, but the true God helps us keep His commands.

His commands are neither hurtful nor grievous. Isn't it a blessing to know the true God?

CHAPTER 7

GOD HAS CHILDREN

As you read through **I John,** you will find words like "brother" and "brethren" popping up again and again. I counted at least 16 times these words appear in five chapters. We are a family. God is making a point. He is not a distant God or an impersonal force or someone distracted and separated from humans. He has children, and He delights in them.

In **Matthew 5, 6 and 7,** we read the Sermon on the Mount which is the first major message of Christ. Notice how Jesus emphasizes the Fatherhood of God. (You will find almost no reference to the Fatherhood of God in the whole Old Testament.) We have a heavenly Father, and we are His children. The true God has a family.

I John 3:1 says,

> *"Behold, what manner of love the Father hath bestowed upon us, that we should be called the sons of God...."*

What a name He gave us! We are sons of God. Let this truth glow in our hearts. Son of God was a name reserved for the angelic beings in the Old

Testament, and now He gives that name to us. I am His son and have all the rights of a son! He is my Father! What manner of love that is! What kind of God would love human beings like you and me and then call us His sons? If He had just let us be His followers, I would have thought that was a privilege. However, He says, *"Come a little closer, and let Me put My arm around you. I am going to be a Father to you, and you are going to be My son."* He lets us be His sons. What a God He is!

I John 3:1-2 reads,

"...therefore the world knoweth us not, because it knew him not. Beloved, now are we the sons of God, and it doth not yet appear what we shall be: but we know that, when he shall appear, we shall be like him; for we shall see him as he is."

These are promises to the sons. We are sons now and will have further blessings in the future.

I John 5:1 says,

"Whosoever believeth that Jesus is the Christ is born of God: and every one

CHAPTER 7: GOD HAS CHILDREN

that loveth him that begat loveth him also that is begotten of him."

We are born—not just adopted or accepted—into God's family. This matter of being "born" and "begotten" is mentioned at least eight times in the book of **I John**. This is not the first birth but a supernatural birth. The true God wants to be known as One that gives birth to sons in His family.

In **John 3:10** Jesus said to Nicodemus,

"Art thou a master of Israel, and knowest not these things?"

In other words, didn't Nicodemus know the true God? Didn't he know God's nature? Didn't he know God's relationship to himself? Didn't he know how God operates? In **verse 7**, Jesus says, *"Ye must be born again."* How could Nicodemus be a master of Israel and not understand this? A lot of people think they get saved by saying a prayer, making a decision, or learning some facts. However, salvation requires a birth. God puts us into His family by birth so that our relationship is close and tight.

I John 5:2 reads,

> *"By this we know that we love the children of God, when we love God, and keep his commandments."*

We are not only the sons born of God, but we are the children of God. If the term *sons* doesn't show us the wonders of belonging to God, maybe the term *children* will.

I John 1:3 describes a little of how God's family operates when it says,

> *"That which we have seen and heard declare we unto you, that ye also may have fellowship with us; and truly our fellowship is with the father, and with his Son Jesus Christ."*

We are not only children of God and sons of God; but when we fellowship, we are all fellowshipping with the Father and His Son. We don't just fellowship on the human level with the children, but we fellowship with our Father. God the Father doesn't cut us off from Himself or leave us alone. He hasn't built a wall between Himself and us. He tries to keep communication lines open. We also need to keep communication lines open so that we can fellowship with Him.

CHAPTER 7: GOD HAS CHILDREN

Enoch walked with God. We ought to want to walk with Him too. We know what it is to fellowship with people, but do we know what it is to fellowship with God? Fellowshipping with God is not just doing right. There were times I was doing right, but I wasn't really fellowshipping with my Father. If we are saved, we are God's sons. (If we are not His sons, we aren't saved.) As sons, we have within us the potential and desire for fellowship. We have a great God that has time to fellowship with us as individuals in our private devotions and as a family in family devotions. He has time to fellowship with us in our prayer times, in our church, and in our work. God has time to fellowship with us all through the day or night, for He desires to fellowship with us. Those times of fellowship with our heavenly Father are such sweet times!

I John 2:18 begins, *"Little children...."* I still talk about my "boys." Mark is the little "boy," and his brother is the bigger "boy." I know they are grown men, but I call them boys. They are both bigger than I am and could whip me. They haven't tried, and I am not eager for them to prove that they could do it. God tells us we are sons. We are His children. He says, *"Little children...."* I like that tender endearment.

The verse goes on to say,

"Little children, it is the last time: and as you have heard that antichrist shall come, even now are there many antichrists; whereby we know that it is the last time."

That was true 1900 years ago. Isn't it even truer today? Our Father in heaven is saying, "Little children, some things that are happening will move you away from my Son Jesus. Some teaching will move you away from knowing Who the true Triune God is. Some teachers will lead you to false christs. You will be in opposition to Who Christ really is." Antichrists, false and counterfeit christs, exist. A lot of people follow them, but the Father doesn't want His children chasing after them. He cares about us, so He warns us. He identifies these antichrists and tries to protect us from them.

I John 2:28 says,

"And now, little children, abide in him; that, when he shall appear, we may have confidence, and not be ashamed before him at his coming."

CHAPTER 7: GOD HAS CHILDREN

God is telling us that when Jesus comes He doesn't want us to be ashamed or embarrassed. We must learn to abide in Christ, to stay faithful, and to walk and do as we have been commanded. If we walk in that fellowship with God, we won't have to be ashamed when Jesus comes. God is warning us to get us ready.

When I was in my upper teens my father would go away for a couple of weeks at a time to Bible conferences and camps. When I was older, I had to tend to our small farm and care for things around home while he was gone. He would tell me when he was leaving and when he would return and leave a list of things he wanted taken care of. I looked at that list. Being an "efficiency expert," I figured out how quickly the list could be done; and I knew how many days of free time I had before I really needed to get to work. When my father did get home, I knew I better have that list done; or I would have to explain why the work had not been completed. We don't know when Jesus is coming, but we do know what His list includes. We know that our heavenly Father didn't leave us a lot of time for idleness or for lying around and enjoying ourselves. We don't want to be ashamed when He comes. He told us how to keep from being ashamed and how to be prepared at all times for His arrival. I like to walk daily so that if Jesus comes, I am up to date on His list. If it is noon, I like to be up to date at noon. If it is night, I like to be up to date before I go to sleep. When Jesus comes, I want to be right with Him and abiding in Him.

What a loving heavenly Father we have. He is not beating us about the ears, driving us, and legalistically trying to corner us. He loves us and cares for us. In mercy and grace, He helps us prepare for Jesus' coming. Oh, I want to be ready; and when I am ready, I want to stay ready. One time when my father was gone, I was to paint the house. I hadn't planned for a rainy day. I hadn't realized that the following day the dew would be around so long. I had to hurry, and I had to prepare my excuses at the same time. We never know what might come up. We want to live ready.

I John 3:7 says,

> ***"Little children, let no man deceive you: he that doeth righteousness is righteous, even as he is righteous."***

Some people are going to lie to us with a straight face and a smile. They are going to speak piously to try to deceive us. Be careful, little children. Some human wolves and skunks are out there.

CHAPTER 7: GOD HAS CHILDREN

I John 3:10 reads,

> *"In this the children of God are manifest, and the children of the devil: whosoever doeth not righteousness is not of God, neither he that loveth not his brother."*

God tells His little children that He wants them to live righteously. Those that don't live righteously don't belong to Him.

I John 4:4 states,

> *"Ye are of God, little children, and have overcome them: because greater is he that is in you, than he that is in the world."*

This is talking about the false spirits. When we get saved, we have to overcome false spirits that will try to keep us from being saved. The devil and his demons will work against our being saved. They will interrupt and redirect our thinking. They will help us think wrongly and make us think that we don't need to repent or that all is right when it isn't. These false spirits will do anything they can to keep us from being saved. When we do get saved, we overcome them. God's little children have overcome them.

We started out in our Christian life overcoming false spirits, and we ought to keep on overcoming them. If we overcame for our own soul, then we will understand how to pray to help others. It takes a man to go into a strong man's house because you have to bind the strong man to spoil his goods **(Mark 3:27)**.

We get passive in our praying sometimes and wonder why not much happens. We must overcome—for those in our family, for those at church, and for the cause of missions. The things about which Robynn and Hannah have testified happened not because they are my daughters but because a wellspring of prayer went up before they ever went to that town in Brazil. We prayed that God would prepare hearts and open doors, and God did precisely that. That is why they have seen what they have seen. What they have seen is not normal in Brazil. In fact, other missionaries have come to see what is happening. Miracles are happening because of overcoming prayer.

Psalm 2:8 says,

"Ask of me, and I shall give thee the heathen for thine inheritance, and the

CHAPTER 7: GOD HAS CHILDREN

uttermost part of the earth for thy possession."

You may say that verse was given to Jesus.

"For all the promises of God in him are yea, and in him Amen, unto the glory of God by us" (II Cor. 1:20).

In the Gulf War, Kuwait was delivered from the hands of Saddam Hussein. A missionary went to Kuwait and started the first gospel witnesses in a totally Muslim country. Those witnesses continue to this day, are self-supporting, and are starting more works. They grew in the confusion immediately after the war. That same missionary may be in Iraq right now. When Iraq wasn't allowing anyone in, he got a visa. When it was not safe for citizens to be there, he went in. He has risked his life to open that country to the gospel. At a time when things couldn't be shipped in, he has gotten Bibles into the country for distribution. God answered prayer and gave five separate and distinct routes by which Bibles could be shipped to a destination in Baghdad. These things couldn't be done unless one knows a God that is greater than he that is in the world. It took prayer to overcome all that demonic activity. The Shiite Muslims are working to rebuild the demonic activity and seize control religiously of that country. We can either fight or let false spirits have Iraq. Because God loves His children, we can overcome false spirits.

"Greater is he that is in you than he that is in the world" (I John 4:4b).

There is an elderly woman that doesn't live far from Hannah's home in Brazil. Hannah started visiting her and read the Scriptures to her. This question arose. Should Hannah continue exposing herself to a practicing witch doctor? I asked, *"Do you think a witch doctor ought to expose herself to the gospel of the Lord Jesus?"* We prayed. It is my understanding that this elderly witch doctor claims to have repented and may have made a profession of salvation. She stopped the witchcraft.

"Greater is he that is in you, than he that is in the world" (I John 4:4b).

We need to march with the true God. We don't march foolishly, brazenly, or temptingly; but we ought to march because we do, in fact, have the true God. He marches with us. We are His children.

CHAPTER 7: GOD HAS CHILDREN

I John 4:6 says,

> *"We are of God: he that knoweth God heareth us; he that is not of God heareth not us. Hereby know we the spirit of truth, and the spirit of error."*

We can get to know each other and know who is in the family of God. I have been in countries where I couldn't speak the language and in situations where there was no translator. I could spot people that belonged to God. We had a common bond. We didn't have to announce to each other, "I am saved. Are you saved?" There was an immediate bond. God lets His children get to know each other and know about each other.

I John finishes by saying,

> *"And we know that the Son of God is come, and hath given us an understanding, that we may know him that is true, and we are in him that is true, even in his Son Jesus Christ. This is the true God, and eternal life. Little children, keep yourselves from idols. Amen"* (I John 5:20-21).

WHO IS THE TRUE GOD?

This is how **I John** closes and how I want to close.

Watch yourself. Be careful that you don't follow that which is not God--an appearance but not reality. Make sure it's the true God that you follow. Keep yourself from idols. Know Who the true God is, and then protect yourself. It will save you a lot of heartache.

INDEX OF WORDS AND PHRASES

1

1900 years ago 92

A

Abraham 22, 23, 44, 49
absolutely 33, 52
absolutely pure 52
Adoniram Judson 68
advocate 33, 65
Alcoholics Anonymous 14
Alexandria, Egypt 59
Allah 7, 28, 67
anointing 25, 40
Antichrists 92
Apostolics 27
arrival 93

B

bankrupt 67
begotten 26, 56, 63, 76, 89
Bitterness 47
Bob 3, 69
Bob Doom 3, 69
born ..23, 35, 47, 53, 56, 63, 72, 76, 88-90
Brazil 96, 98
broke their hearts 54
brother 7, 33, 47, 53, 55, 61, 72, 80, 87, 91, 95
Buddhists 8

C

camps 93
Charles Spurgeon 68
children 7, 15, 25, 33, 53, 55, 65, 72, 73, 80, 83, 87, 90-92, 94-96, 98, 99
cleanses 21
closer 20, 88
coin 67
Commander 84
commands 14, 79, 80, 81, 83, 85
community 36, 74, 75
conferences 93, 110
confess 29, 50, 65
Confucians 8
congregation 80
conspiracies 73
created 22, 23, 26, 85
creation 22, 26

D

Daniel 46, 76, 110
darkness 17, 45-48, 80
day of judgment 55
deist 26
den of lions 76
devil 7, 20, 21, 28, 33, 53, 56, 59, 66, 72, 74, 76, 95
disregard 27, 46

divorce 42
drunken man 75
Dwight Moody 68

E

embarrassed 93
Enoch 17, 91
errors 64
eternal life 8, 19, 23, 32, 35, 36, 99
Eve 7
evil spirit 29
example 20, 29, 48, 68, 82

F

false 7, 9, 14, 37, 85, 92, 95, 96, 98
false spirits 95, 96, 98
farm 93
fellowship 16, 17, 19, 30, 31, 45-47, 65, 90, 91, 93
foundational 15
friend 28
funnel 68
furnace 76

G

George Mueller 68
Georgia 61
gesture 80
god . 7, 9, 14, 18, 36, 41, 42, 57, 62, 63, 67

God bestows His love 60
God is light 45
God is one 27
God is three 27
Godhead 25
Gomorrah 49
good person 33
great teacher 33
Greenville, SC 66
guilt 21, 54
Gulf War 97
gun 75

H

Hannah 96, 98
hate 18, 27, 67
His name's sake 66
Holy .. 23, 25, 27, 29, 30, 33, 35, 39, 40, 43, 54
holy life 44, 70
honest 44
hope 24, 51, 52, 67, 83
Hudson Taylor 68

I

idols 7, 12, 99, 100
immoral 42
impersonal force 87
incarnation 19, 23
indwelling 25, 30
intellectually 31
Iraq 97

INDEX OF WORDS AND PHRASES

J

James Stewart 69
Joseph 76
judgment 56

K

knocking at a door 52
Koran 14
Kuwait 97

L

learn 11, 14, 17, 18, 70, 93
legal lawyer 33
lies 42, 43, 46, 76, 81
light ... 11, 17, 45-47, 65, 77, 80
literally 31
love 7, 17, 18, 20, 26, 28, 33, 34, 43, 55, 59-64, 71, 73, 79, 82, 83, 87, 88, 90
love of God is perfected 59

M

man upstairs 79
manner 60, 62, 87, 88
marks 8, 9, 30
Methodist 36
millions 110
Miracles 96
missions 61, 63, 96, 110
modified Santa Claus 57
Mormons 7, 27
Morrow 62

Muslims 7, 26, 28, 97
mysterious 26

N

nature 11, 24, 33, 39, 40, 42, 43, 46, 49, 50, 66, 82, 84, 85, 89
neighbors 36
neutral 48
never sinned 39
Nicodemus 89

O

obedient 81
Ohio 36, 110
Ord Morrow 62
Origen 59

P

pastor 42, 52, 110
pathway 20
Pharaoh 76
poem 42
potato 48
power of holiness 44
prayer .16, 67, 68, 89, 91, 96, 97
pre-existence 23
principal 36
promises 70, 88, 97
propitiation 34, 35, 63, 65
Purgatory 34
purge 66

103

R

representative 33
reveals 11-15, 17, 21, 24, 26, 27, 30, 34, 36
revelation 13, 16, 17, 30, 36
righteously 95
Robert Murray McCheyne 44
Robynn 96

S

Sabbath 85
Saddam Hussein 97
Salvation 16
Scotland 69
seconds 13
secret enemies 49
separate 18, 31, 35, 97
Seventh Day Adventists 7, 35
Shadrach, Meshach, and Abednego 76
Shiite 97
skunks 94
Sodom 49
some . 15, 18, 33, 41, 48, 53, 54, 59, 66, 67, 71, 80, 84, 85, 89, 92
Son 8, 16, 17, 19, 21, 26- 35, 43-45, 63, 65, 72, 82, 87, 90, 92, 99
spiritist 74, 75
stolen 54
strange and mysterious ways 42

strictness of God 49
struggles 66
Suffering and glory go together 84
suicide 75
supernatural birth 89

T

themes 8, 35
Thomas Jefferson 26
tongues 74
translator 99
Triune God ... 27, 29, 34, 36, 40, 92
tri-unity 27
trouble 9, 79
true .. 7-9, 11, 14, 16-20, 22, 25, 26, 28, 30, 32-37, 46, 50, 52, 57, 60, 62- 64, 73, 75-77, 80, 84, 85, 87, 89, 92, 98, 99, 100
truth and is no lie 40
truth-telling man 44

U

unholy 39
Unitarians 27
unity 29, 31
up to date 94

V

victory 34

INDEX OF WORDS AND PHRASES

vomit 54

W

warlocks 74
washes 21
weary 46
what a day that will be 24
William Carey 68
witch doctor 98
Witches 74

witness of God 35, 43
wolves 94
Word. 12-14, 16, 19, 27, 30, 59, 70, 77
Word of God .12, 13, 16, 30, 70
world 17, 18, 23, 24, 26, 29, 34, 40, 41, 55, 56, 59-63, 65, 73, 74, 88, 95, 97, 98
worldly Christian 18

ABOUT THE AUTHOR

J. PAUL RENO has been a pastor in Ohio and Maryland since 1968. During this time he has also been involved in church planting, training men for the ministry and speaking on mission fields in Europe, the Middle East, Africa, South America and Mexico. The church he presently pastors has sent millions of dollars to missions. He continues to speak at various Bible conferences, camp meetings and local churches. He presently serves on the Board of Directors for the Conversion Center, which is headquartered in Hagerstown, Maryland. Pastor Reno recently was honored with the prestigious award, "Defender of the Scriptures," by the King James Bible Research Council.

He is also the author of *To Fight or Not to Fight*, *Daniel Nash: Prevailing Prince of Prayer*, *Investing for Eternity*, *Studies in Bible Doctrine* as well as over fifty pamphlets and booklets on salvation, the Christian life, Bible doctrine and the King James Version. His wife,

Carolyn authored *Almost But Lost*, available as a free ebook download at:

http://www.theoldpathspublications.com/Pages/Free.htm.

www.ingramcontent.com/pod-product-compliance
Lightning Source LLC
Chambersburg PA
CBHW061452040426
42450CB00007B/1329